Foreword

It is with great pleasure
admiration that I was invited to say four words (I got carried away or misinterpreted the assignment) to introduce this poetry compilation, a testament to the vibrant and diverse voices of Tokyo. As a part-time patron of the arts and a unwitting supporter of creative expression in all its forms, it is truly an honor to witness the culmination of poetic brilliance showcased within these pages.

It was a dark and stormy night, nights tend to be dark but welcome to an eclectic and varied collection of far brighter poetry spoken from the heart of Tokyo's long standing pub, What The Dickens! Within these pages lies a rich tapestry of human emotion, woven by The Four Prose of The Apostrophe; Andy, Ade, Quenby, and Eri, They say if you read this in silence you can almost here them pronounce their Oxford commas. Through evocative verses, these poets transcend ink and paper, inviting you into the very soul of the city and themselves. Their lyrical alchemy captures the essence of love, loss, and longing, forming a symphony of words that echoes betwixt the wood lined walls.

What makes the What The Dickens open mic sessions special is the sense of community fostered within its walls. It is a haven for poets, both seasoned and novice, to share their innermost thoughts and feelings without fear of judgment but rather with the expectation of understanding and solidarity. This book serves as a testament to that spirit of camaraderie, as these four poets come together to offer a collective voice, a chorus of souls united in the pursuit of truth and beauty.

To the readers embarking on this literary journey, I urge you to approach these poems with an open heart and a receptive mind. Allow yourself to be transported to the cobblestone streets of Tokyo, to feel the pulse of the city coursing through your veins, and to hear the echoes of applause reverberating in your ears. For within these verses lie not just words, but worlds waiting to be explored and emotions waiting to be felt.

May this compilation serve as a beacon of inspiration for aspiring poets everywhere and a reminder of the transformative power of art. And may the voices of Andy, Ade, Quenby, and Eri continue to echo through the hallowed halls of What The Dickens, enriching the lives of all who have the privilege to hear them. I will leave you to enter the realm of the spoken words contained herein with this quote.

"Do all the good you can, by all the means you can, in all the ways you can, in all the places you can, at all the times you can, to all the people you can, as long as ever you can."
John Wesley (1703 -1791)

John Cole

Ade Crawley

From the UK, but left to travel the world in 1991, never to return (well yet anyway), just had too much fun. Along the way had many heart breaks, adventures, tears and laughter, and discovered at a late age that his random writings were actually something people wanted to hear! Loves playing his guitar, cooking, walking his dog, spending time with his wife and watching his children mature into amazing people.

Slipping Away

The hardest thing for me today
Is watching you slowly slip away

A child of the 30's, wartime teenage beauty
A midlands girl wooed by yankee flyers
Met a man called Donald, danced the night away
Created a big family, children, grandchildren
Spread your love into the world, a dynasty of teachers
Now slowly drifting away, like a child

Watching from afar makes me feel so selfish
Wondering if my future looks like this

The hardest thing for me today
Is the prospect I'll never see you again

Standing, crying

Saying goodbye to you, ten years on
A shaking of shoulders, a sobbing sound
Reading your poems, a cold wind blows
It's easier to say I love you when you aren't alive to listen

The modality of depression

I Should
I Could
I Would
I May
I Might
I Shall

I will do something today, I really will!

Something

Today

Maybe!

In my mind I replied

In my mind I replied

To the message about your brother
It was full of pain and made me sad
I tried to comfort you
I said it will get better
I wanted to share your pain
To make you see the sun again
I created a wonderful story
To make you feel all homely
It mentioned all your good points
And ignored all the stumbling blocks
It was a fantastic message
It would have made you feel much better

In my mind I replied

NBD

Its 9PM on a Sunday night and the national bank of daddy is a busy place, tickets for Disney (credit card please), bills for Juku (more more more), flights to Korea (it's for university), more more more,

The national bank of daddy is open once again, no withdrawal too big, never closes the door

Even if the money in doesn't match the money out, the requests for bank of daddy help will never ever relent

It's as if the rest of them think money grows on trees, glad they never get to see the account reality

The money over twenty years is like two shiny Ferrari Not something they tell you when you get down on one knee

The national bank of daddy, is open every day, given other options would it open up again?

My Stuff

It's my stuff- leave it alone
It doesn't matter if it looks a mess
it's mine, it's mine
It's not for you to decide
it's mine, it's mine
If it goes in the rubbish bin, it's my decision to make
it's mine, it's mine
Policing everything you throw away, can't trust you anymore.
No respect for *my* property
it's mine, it's mine

Husband Really?

I'm going to be the best sodai gomi in town
If that's what you think I am
Good to know my place
A useful household addition
A wallet with a face
Great for cooking, cleaning, washing,
But don't take up too much space

Your just some sodai gomi
Keep going, at your pace

Taking a brief interlude to create some beautiful space in my own simple way

Gives me the energy to be the best sodai gome in town today

Permanent Impermanence

A brief interlude of beauty on a barren tree
Green leaves waiting, petals for us to see
A culture based on permanent impermanence oxymoron oddity
Always wanting new, and fresh, yet respecting elderly
Mutually exclusive concepts make people slightly uneasy
As beers are drunk and petals fall another start is seen

And as usual the rain and wind make viewing less than easy

A cold night, a fleeting glimpse of permanent impermanent beauty.

Tarquin 250 Love bunnies

In an Eastern land, there's a band you need to meet

Their pounding sound is so irresistibly unique

Tarquin 250 Lovebunnies

They'll make you feel alive

Quirky beats are lively, melodies divine

A melange of genres, a sound so fine

Tarquin 250 Lovebunnies

Their energy contagious, their passion quite untold

The stories smack of poetry, lyrics sound so real

Listening to them really is like a spiritual meal

They're a band of incongruity, a band of love

Tarquin 250 Lovebunnies, they could be here to stay

Their earworms will linger, long after they've gone away

Bankers with a W

In the world of high finance, another crisis did arise

The banking system faltered, as it took us by surprise

Fear swept across the land as banks couldn't stand

The many suffered because of the greed of a few

Reckless risk profited them a lot, the rest of us just lost

The fallout was harsh, and the pain was real

People lost their homes and jobs, trust was shattered and broken

And those responsible delayed their yachts by 18 months

A government bailout intervened, to save what they could

But the damage was done, the wound was deep

The scars of the crisis, forever to keep

Haneda, oh where did you go

A corridor of a thousand shouts

Got to get your smartphone out

Blue screen, blue screen, let me see

Go here, go there, chaos to me

Disorganized, over staffed, who is arranging this?

Throw bodies at a problem and a greater one exists

Oh calm and clear Haneda, where did you go

Waiting for the call you never want

I hope you never go there
The place where waiting hurts
Knowing that you cannot stop
The reality of what they've got
It eats away as time counts down
The pain of knowing there won't be one more time

And distance means you cannot touch, try to express
that you love so much

Waiting for the call you never want
Ever present pain defines each day
Knowing the pain won't go away

Waiting for the call you never want

Authors and Poets

Authors write, poets construct, but categorize not me
My head thinks this is bullshit
My dream is to be free

Teenage Angst - (I think I wrote this in 1982)

There must be a reason for all this madness in my mind
The feelings that I can't describe
Nothing prepares you for life like this
You can't decide, don't want to decide

Sometimes things seem clear, but those are soon forgotten
Something seems like losing part of your life
The questions fly around the neurons
Why? What? If?

It's only life, it will not change
You can't pretend to yourself that it ended
Just a part of yourself has ceased to be a constant
Songs seem melancholic, dreams are scary
Unable to rationalize, three weeks of pain
A burning inside

Part wanting to leave, the rest too lazy to move
Came here for a reason, put my thoughts on paper
Other's find a flow of words, mine are simply stilted

Constant interruptions, constant pain
Alcohol soothes but ultimately confuses

And yet I survived!

It's hard to be a pop star (the first song I wrote)

It's hard to be a pop star
When no one knows your name
It's hard to be a pop star
When they think you play the same game
They don't want to let you in
They don't want to let you sing
So you have to stand outside
And play to the passers by

It's so hard

It's so hard to be what you want to be
They don't want to let you smile
They shatter your illusions
Make you wait outside

It's so hard

Happiness

Have I been happy? Oh many times
I travelled the world, saw happiness inducing incredible sights
Watching the clouds fall over the mountains around Lake Toba
Moonlit nights on Perhentian Kecil watching the turtles lay their eggs
Temples in the clouds of Xishuangbanna, fields of butterflies
The taste of a baozi in Chongqing market
Pho in Cu Chi, banana leaf curry in JB
Tacos and cerveza as the waves crash in Puerto Escondido
Tamale in Antigua, sunrise over Tikal
Yes - happiness has inhabited me so many times you see.

I sate my happiness sitting in bars, singing songs, having a yarn
People smiling, music playing
Happiness is always saying, that I love you, to the ones you love; that I care - if their life is run.

The first kiss of your child, a miraculous feeling, happiness surging, hardly breathing, a feeling of immense responsibility, wrapped in happiness enveloped me.

But age tempers happy thoughts, as issues bring me down constantly
It would be better to ignore the news that's beating at my door.
Maybe happiness you see, is not noticing what's going on around

Please don't dismiss me as a pedant to suggest, if I dare
That true happiness is the privilege of the socially unaware

The end before another beginning

August the twelfth
Seventy six days
Until the footy starts again
We watched you play your final games,
Not much to decide apart from a couple to drop
Of these teams I cared not a lot
Mine were safe in a mediocre location
Glory skipped us
Programmes folded
Tears of joy rehoused in boxes
Waiting to burst out as summer wanes
In seventy six days
Another footy year

When Lying Counts

It took a while to realize, but when I did I cried inside
It wasn't that you went with them that hurt my heart so brittle/thin
It was the fact you looked at me and lied
When you did a part inside me died

The signs were there for many years, but I rejected all my fears
That you could have a separate box, full of secrets, hard and soft
Other people's words caressing, hands possessing, pleasure getting
Without any of my love to see

I do accept you're free, can't control you see
Just need to know you're always there for me, endlessly

When lying counts you realize the feelings that you have inside
There is a place we all should go, where pain & pleasure mingle so

I wish your heart good luck when this you see.

When that day you see

Good luck your heart from me

When that day you see

Good luck your heart from me

In Praise Of Average

Nothing wrong with being average
The majority of us are
We don't need to be excellent
At thoughts, actions or deeds
Just provide for yourself and family
As best you can
Respect your environment
As best you can
Be nice to your fellow
As best you can

Average is normal, regular, it's sound
It allows the hyper motivated to shine, make waves, be Alpha, end up dead on Everest or at the bottom of the sea

I think I'll keep being average for me!

Splat

It's that time of year again where we have the same old battle
You trying to sneak past my defences, me constantly checking
I spray myself with deet, cover my ample meat, try to cut down my CO_2, So I can walk around, and you will never know
But your senses are finely tuned, you sneak onto my skin
And if I spot you there I have a millisecond to swipe
And splat - you cease to be a mite!

Shorts

Roses - these I would have got
Love - I gave a little
Pride - was my great temporer
You only had me smitten

I looked away, you gave no more
The thing just had to end
Conscious decisions have gone girl
Just the feelings of a friend

Forcing me to move
Shaking back and forth
The train is like my heart
An unbecoming force

At Berkhampstead I wrote a note
It makes no sense to me
OK it rhymes and moves in time
But can it make me free?

We Tried

We tried, we tried so hard but couldn't conceive
A subject friends will drop at meals
Nobody wants to make amends
Avoid the topic, an elephant shadow at the end
Watching others walk by with children, always brings
a jolt of remorse
We tried, we tried so hard, but it was not to be

Please, please enjoy your family

The Orange One

Don't want to gloat, but he's going down, he's going to suffer the pain of a fall
The master of fake it till you make it, a rich boy with a history of failed business

Well, if you can't make money from a casino
Then you aren't really in business are you

If he'd taken his legacy money at 21, invested it and sat on a beach in the sun

He'd now have more

Pass the popcorn, this is going to be good!

I got it

Finally after fifty years
I've found the answer to all my fears
Something beautiful, and smooth and fine
That always makes me happy, all the time
It never makes me feel guilty, it makes me smile
The answer to my stresses, it took so long to find
Nothing that came from advice from parents, friends or muses
It takes me to a better place
It's available in many forms
You can get it at the corner
Walking home with sores
It's wonderful fantastic
It slips down oh so well
The answer to your problems, do you want me to tell?

It's brown, and sweet and mine

I'll eat chocolate all the time!

A Bad Month

You're not any different from anyone else
Sometimes your organization falls off the shelf
Meetings are missed, projects forgotten
Just be happy it isn't so often
And hope that the others don't take it too badly
Get stroppy or angry or shout in a frenzy
As we all have a bad week or month now and then
Try to stay positive as the bad month will end

What you want

You want passion, but you want me to be gentle
You want me to be creative, but demand that I provide
You need companionship, yet stare at your screen
Advice is ignored, accusations thrown
You want everything and nothing
Want to go everywhere, but nowhere

So you do you, and I'll do me
Maybe that will create a pleasant harmony

A New Life

I had a dream last night
I met the woman of my dreams
She had a son who looked at me
As I was standing in the loo
He had a dirty mark on his face
I make a remark, he smiled
Outside he said to his mum 'he's a nice guy'
She smiled at me and my heart stopped beating, my mouth became a pit of dryness and my words failed
'Take me to the Red Lion' she said
I couldn't, but I passed her my card
'I live in Tokyo' I said
She smiled and said 'well I will get a lot of air miles then'
The look between us could have reduced Everest to a mere dust pile
I saw a world of possibilities in her smile

A new life

The only problem now is how do I explain this to my wife?

Friendships

What makes a friend to you?

School friends from a very young age with shared emotional experiences?
Fleeting friends from a certain point where your feeling was delirious?
Work friends from a stressful job, you ganged up on the terrible boss?
People living down your street, who friended you as you walked your beat?
Facebook friends you rarely know, but linked up once a long time ago?
The friend of the darkness who visits you at night? A being designed to give your fright?
A lonely speaker in a foreign bar seeking friends who have travelled so very far?

What makes a friend to you?

Procrastiwot?

I was going to read an article
It said that procrastination is a response to long term depression
The catch copy said it's a result of previous trauma
It wants me to click on the link

I'm just too unhappy to be bothered at the moment!

Almost Empty

For twenty years I've been providing, cooking
cleaning, washing, wiping

And now the end of rearing, a new direction steering
Hobby time expanding, money slightly less lacking

A bittersweet feeling of impending freedom
Time with a partner, time for conversations

But always in my mind a feeling
Watching over, subtly steering

Go forth and fly my progeny

Love you always, please live free.

The Full Moon Blues

Woke up at 3 AM
Heavy in the head
Something pushed me up
And out of bed
Wandered past my dog, snoring like a train
Looked out the window, expecting lots of rain

Instead I saw a bright light shining down on me
Unhappy feelings flooded in you see

I got the full moon blues
The full moon blues,
Hep me get away from these full moon blues

Monthly nightime prowlings
Gravity you see
Is having lots of negative
Effects on me
Want to feel a happiness, want to smile and sing
But the weight of that big lump of rock is crushing down on me

I got the full moon blues

The full moon blues

Hep me get away from these full moon blues

Another Child

We sit and swipe the evening news
Attacks incursions, guns and planes
To many it appears to be the same
Electric war in easy bites
Watching people try to fight
Against a technology far superior
But don't critique or you will be
Cancelled as anti-Jew you see
What are we wilting liberals now supposed to be

And as you drink and laugh and play
Another child in Palestine dies today
Another father/mother screams in pain, a brother's
blood screams the same
Anger gilded in their minds
The next generation of revenge is set in time

Another child breathes their last
And Western countries tie their flags to the mast of
fighting back against terrorism
Addled by fifty years of indifference

When it was said in late 80's
Your creating the next generation of enemies
By fighting intifada rocks with live rounds
And watching from afar

Nothing was done by the powers at the bar
Drinking, happy, smiling in their life
Sated in the knowledge we're not there

And Tehran and Tel Aviv have hawks a plenty
Protected by the power of thousands of M4s
They send in other's children to fight their dirty wars

And so another child dies, in the chaos known as Palestine

Thank you for sharing

Weekday evening
Tired from work
Thirty minutes of complete escape for me
You took me to your coffee shop
Cracked sarcastic wit a lot
Totally unrealistic lifestyles in a big city
Had more time to talk than work
Simple scandals, family stuff
And kept it together as a group of friends
Made us cry at the very end
And as you cross the rainbow bridge
A world of memes about your wit
Your awkwardness resonated in me
I saw a kindred spirit you see
Addictive personalities alike to be
Need companions to stop us going to extremes

And it ended, you drifted away, to a million dollar mansion and endless empty days

And through it all you said to us

I'll be there for you

Do do……

Life's a Beach

That warmth, you can't really describe

Reminds you of a safer time, when mum and dad looked after you, on a beach, in a place with deck chairs and candy floss

Sand gets in between your toes, it comes home to remind you weeks after, you smile a little as you remember, the warmth on your back, the sounds of the sea

Life's a beach, a happy place, where you don't really need to be stressed, worried, frightened much

A place of such beauty you smile all over

And after, as you walk dark streets, of rainy towns the beach remembers you

Whoosh…..

You're seven years old, looking at yourself in a mirror, friends are waiting outside to play….whoosh

At twelve the hormones are flowing and you feel all confused… whoosh

Sixteen and you have your first kiss, hoping to get more like this .. whoosh

Twenty three and living hard, still no cash but it's great having a wild time…… whoosh

Twenty nine and life is tough, just don't seem to have enough, time or money or friends of hope… whoosh

And then you meet a wonderful person, set down roots and start to get serious…whoosh

A child is born, your sleep forgotten, life is frantic, never boring….whoosh

Two decades pass, where did they go? The kids leave home and you turn to see, a person you remember, but do they remember me…whoosh

And the realization you only have 15 summers to go…whoosh, whoosh, whoosh

I Don't Speak Grunt

I'm lucky to have travelled
Have seen a hundred lands
Communicated badly, often with my hands
But the most challenging of times you see
Are when teenagers talk to me
They have a different mode of speech
One which utterly confuses
I thought it was my issue until I realized one day

I don't speak grunt.

I don't do shrug
Can't understand 'whatever'
Rolling eyes means nothing to me
A word you see is what I need
When questions are asked
Responses are required
With less of a 'huh' or an evil side eye

Waiting for that magical moment
When fluid language flows
You must be wanting something
Money I suppose

Please remember when you speak
A row of words is what I seek
I'll try to understand you if I can

But I don't speak grunt

Perching

Sometimes I listen to lyrics of songs
And imagine the background that brought them along
As Steven sang about life on the edge
In my mind I could see
A person on a tightrope
Balancing life as they see
Between living happy, single and free
Or married, and stressed, with bills as far as you can see

But I was wrong, it wasn't a battle between married or single
He was singing about his bed and the space so little
As I lie perched on my 15 percent
I wonder who else could be taking up my bed
She's smaller than me, but spreads oh so well
That 75 percent is covered up swell

So as I lie perched on the edge of my bed
In jumps the dog, and there goes my head
And off to the sofa I wearily creep
It's not much to ask for some space for a sleep

And they wonder why I get tired before 6PM

If I slept in 75%

I wouldn't

Andy Boerger

Andy is a long time Tokyo resident from Ohio, an artist who discovered his writing voice by arguing with people about the existence of God on Richard Dawkins' blog (he took the 'aye' position). Poetry came much later, growing out of his love for writing lyrics. He still can't figure out what 'poet' means but is reasonably sure he's earned the right to wear that cap.

The Fall of Empires

the ornament was made of the finest, most delicate Venetian Glass
it was light as a feather
it gave off a history vibe when you cradled it in your palm
you danced with the Romanovs wined with the Hapsburgs
it fell and shattered; tiny shards fell onto every wrapped gift beneath the tree
such that one could not touch a present without cutting oneself
and so the gifts went unopened and simply remained there
with the blood and the history
until it was time to take the tree away

Superhero

He was her superhero,

lit her sun cleared her skies

made rainbows dance before her eyes

he became her supervillain,

brought the flood of tears

from eyes that would behold

no more rainbows

Halloween

Things are not as they seem
terrors lurk below, unseen
sounds that set your hair on edge
sanity pushed to the ledge
what was that? A raven's wings
or flapping of more frightening things?
I fear that Death is at my door
what am I resisting for?
a child's blood flows forth like wine
on blackest streets of Palestine
this Halloween

Rashomon Test

We are all Rorscharch Tests to one another
Your you, my you, and somebody else's you are
different people completely
My me, your me, and someone else's me are as well;
Like the self-justifying protagonists of 'Rashomon'
we don't see the truth; we represent it
This goes all the way back to the beginning
If my mother had been different
if my father had stuck around
the Rorscharch test of you would appear differently
concave perhaps where now convex
Less threatening, perhaps
less like a dragon more like an angel
If I appear more dragon-like than angelic to you
please squint your eyes tight
Look again give me another chance
and I will do the same

Spirits

Much more frightening than spirits is the spirit of
wanting to expunge the world of spirits;
and those who insist that we all must see the world
as they see it
as nuts and bolts properties and formulae equations
and effects;
skeptics/atheists who insist that spirit has no place in
science
no place to haunt in this world
everything is dead dead dead
meaningless
even your consciousness is very probably an illusion
and only the deluded and ignorant could possibly
think otherwise
BOO! They are the ones who scare me

Untitled

The Sea covers three quarters of the planet's surface
but with barely more than an apple skin of thickness
and yet this thin coat this barely there veil of wetness
over granite authors the whole story of life on Earth;
We call the sea Mother; we taste Her in our sweat
and tears; we plunge into her like babes longing to
reclaim the womb as home;
in the chatter of seagulls we hear 'Om'

Lopsided

Relationships can die
but their ghosts haunt social media such that their
mournful echo may arise unexpectedly and
suddenly; for example, when looking at past posts
from a new friend, a face may appear
a smiling face, having a good time in a video you are
in and your new friend who was nothing more than
an acquaintance at the time is in
and the happy face is of someone who loved you at
the time and no longer does
and they are seated there mere feet away from your
new friend
It is sad.
Because the memories of the relationship are now
lopsided. The disappointment and the heartache
and the tragedy having tilted it over

~ mid 20th century message

At the first sign of environmental catastrophe you must take action
this is vitally important
It will mean hard decisions, politically, economically
it will involve sacrifices up and down the economic totem pole
the rich will need to help the poor
the nations that have already squandered their own resources must be willing to help those who still have resources to protect;
saving your rainforests - that's going to be key
You MUST keep those oxygen factories running
preserving your atmosphere, keeping balance
You will need to do something about your extraction/consumption based society
it is a recipe for disaster and you will realize this sooner rather than later
you will need to listen to the visionaries among your academics who preach that small is beautiful
The first signs mean already you are in trouble

your problems have only begun

but ignoring them is not an option

unless you are an insane species that has no interest in survival

Just remember this: the first signs are when you get started, no delays and you'll be okay

Lust

knowing that she was being worshipped
or at least part of her was
didn't hurt matters
adulation being the greatest aphrodisiac
thus, she willingly if not to say obediently
jutted her plump velvety fruity and oh so round
derriere
before the gaze of her slavish admirer ready to feel....
the brush
Over wine they had discussed the matter
he had shown her his rough sketches
 'You're crazy!' she laughingly taunted him
knowing that he knew she could simply pass on his
request
as a female bowerbird might turn away from a
forlorn suitor's masterpiece
'I think we're both crazy', was his reply
and with a wink the point was conceded assent was
given
He had chosen Munch's 'The Scream'

he felt somewhat brilliantly
the round globular face
the undulating brushstrokes of the background
surely this theme and this 'canvas' was a match made in heaven
Midway through the artist realized he needed something more tactile
so brushes were abandoned as finger painting took over
smearing, pressing, blending touch/flesh/press/caress until the famous painting came to life in 3D!
Finally came the frame
perfectly chosen to fit without falling
with just enough squeezing and extension of the glutes
He looked, with the greatest satisfaction an artist can know upon his masterpiece
he had planned it, dreamed it, imagined it desired it
and now it perkily wobbled before him
blocking out all cares of a lifetime
she looked back at him saw the rapture in his face
and winked again

cliffhanger

as cliffhangers go this one is a doozy
we are at the edge or maybe two edges
or maybe even three
we stand at a precipice of utter environmental
devastation
the engineering of a planet that can no longer
support our civilization
possibly even our species
we just kept walking until we got here
meanwhile, we stare over another cliff where our
inventions have become so sophisticated that they
threaten our civilization in another way
ending the concept of livelihood/profession/
employment while siphoning all value
into the bank accounts of a sliver of the populace
while increasing exponentially
their power to control the masses
they laugh at us
they warned us about this in movies and novels
while marching us here against our will

'well, what are you going to do about it?'
they sneer through their cackles
and then there is yet another
related to the others, but dangerous enough on its
own we stare into an abyss of complete economic
collapse because our system, 'capitalism'
is not actually a system at all
unsustainable/inequitable/exploitative/rapacious
not a system but a MAW
and so here we are
the suspense is killing me
it is killing you as well
What Happens Next??

Amnesia

When the Soul Guides weren't looking
she spit out the mouthful of water from The Fountain
of Amnesia
they had instructed her to swallow
so she returned to Earth with full memory of her past
lives
This complicated her life when she met those who
had previously abused her
who came back as siblings, dorm mates and
coworkers
she could barely contain her rage
barely restrain herself from striking them, or worse

When she linked up again with those whom SHE had
harmed
she was always brought to tears
that she of course could not explain
sometimes she would come into their rooms at night
as they were sleeping and silently beg for their
forgiveness as she wept

A 'normal' life was not possible for her, clearly
she became a New Age healer
but she barely charged enough for her services to survive
what right had she to enrich herself simply because she had misbehaved in the Bardo while her clients had dutifully done as instructed?

She understood it all
why she was terrified of boats
why she binge watched horror movies alone when all her candles had gone out
why she was a lesbian
why she was musically gifted
especially why it was so hard to relate to others, or to trust them

Still, she was not unhappy
she regretted many of her actions and decisions from past lives
but she DIDN'T regret disobeying her Soul Guides

She liked seeing her life as a kind of three dimensional chess board
it was as if she were the only one who understood a cubist painting
or could hear the beauty in an avant garde musical composition
She knew, of course, that her Guides knew
she wondered if they found her naughty
she knew that, soon enough, she would be with them again
would she follow the rules this time?
She decided she would cross that bridge when she came to it

inappropriate

We understand that you love Leonore very much
and that she loves you very much
we understand that no one is harmed by your
displays of love toward one another
we understand that in your later years, and after
having lost Ruth so long ago
it is a great treasure to you that your needs
so long unfulfilled
are being met
In our way, we are happy for you and Leonore
she seems perfectly content with the situation
by all accounts she is as happy
as she could possibly be
her eyes shine bright, she is playful and affectionate
her devotion to you is palpable
she is beautiful from the tip of her snout to
the tip of her tail
She too, after all, has been alone all these years and
nobody denies that her kind too has needs

However, we draw the line at what you are proposing
we will not report you to the authorities
but neither will we attend your 'wedding'
we feel it's Inappropriate

Tokyo

Tokyo assaults the senses insults the eardrums onslaughts the eyeballs ambushes the nostrils flaunts its modernity struts its sterility shouts its imbecility vaunts its virility parades its enormity waltzes like a wannabe fan-dances its history cancans its cacophony plants itself on a fault line like a canary in a coal mine what, you ask, is that a sign that Fuji is erupting?

addiction

She was addicted to lions
she started watching 'The Lion King' at four
that was her gateway
'started watching' because four year olds can watch
beloved movies every day and twice on Sundays
she loved everything about that movie
but especially she loved the lions
and she loved everything about the lions
but especially she loved their manes
Those manes!
how they captured her child's mind
she became obsessed with them and wanted to
know them more
what did they smell like? she wondered and
wondered. she wanted to bury her head in the mane
of a lion and smell
From there it was monthly visits to the Safari Park
her parents indulged her
it was a sacrifice; those parks aren't cheap and they
had their fill of them after one or two visits

but it was rare to see a child so fixated on something
at such a young age
and who knows? They may have had a Jane Goodall
on their hands
but the Safari Park only filled her with more longing
she couldn't get close enough
couldn't touch the lions/smell their manes
so she moved to Africa
she quit her job, spent all her money
set up a tent, and began living near the lions
The lions sensed there was nothing to fear from her
nothing to lose by letting her be among them
so she stayed with the lions and each night she
buried her head in the mane of the pride leader
and smelled
and dreamed dreams no human sounds entered

A group came from Hollywood
they wanted to make a reality show about her
she sent them away; they had nothing to offer her
nothing that interested her
they were merely vulgar, and repellant

after a few years she no longer could be easily
recognized as human
not a lion either
she was a singular creature of this Earth
and then one day the lions devoured her
the way of all addictions

Crosswalk

At the crosswalk there is always a great gathering
discussions of profound importance continually take
place there
Decisions are made/ decisions are regretted
decisions are deferred to further up the road
Animals/people Extraterrestrials/fictional characters
the dead/the living shamans/priestesses trees
sorting through the chatter can be maddening but
not purposeless
Which way will you go? Which way will you go?

escape

escape = landscape? beachwaterfallforestriver place outside steel cities, where birds sing louder than traffic

escape = mindscape? miracle of words on a page, immersion mystery solvers, warriorsloversheroesvillainstyrantsmonsters
chance to involve myself with others who know not of me and ask for nothing

escape = space? tech visionaries say follow me I have more money than you so you must listen when I tell you we must prepare to escape from this home planet that we ourselves have made inhospitable it's the only way

escape = peace? what threatens us, that we need escape?
fold, then, into that aspect of you that cannot be threatened

the buddhachristkingdomcrownchakra of liberation

Journey

the journeyer approached the desert with fear
hollow before him, empty as the sky
lifeless as the moon, dry as the brittle wisps of hair
that clung to the head of his grandmother as she lay
on her deathbed long ago
Not to cross was no option, as the desert grew daily
waiting it out was a fool's game
eventually the desert would find him
better to do things on his own terms
cross it ~ that was the only way.
He would not follow the trail of skeletons
though that was the advice he had received
 'follow the trail of skeletons, but take more rations
and be hardier than they and you may succeed
where they failed'.
instead, he would make his own route rather than
follow a doomed path
the desert might whittle him down to a skeleton as it
had done all the others but again, it might not

the desert tempted him with mirages, drove him
mad with heat
humiliated him into drinking his own piss
but then
just before the last remaining molecule of his will
evaporated in the mocking heat he heard, in the
distance
waves as they fell upon a shore

Untitled

the pendulum sways between the creative swirling
brazenness of divinity and the oil/soil stickiness of
humanity
there, in the center the all watching Eye

hush

In the hush we can hear the Song of the body merge with the gently buzzing electricity that lives within us feel its impulse as it rises from the base of the spine gathers melody as it ascends, blooms chorus-like as it fills our shoulders and resounds extending beyond the dome of our head; holding there, symphonic I AM ALIVE HALLELUJAH I AM ALIVE
In the hush the clutter of thoughts gives way to the stillness of presence; awareness that doesn't scramble for defining labels, that doesn't tell ANY stories; just is
In this hush the Self is known beyond personhood beyond form: I AM DIVINE CREATIVITY eternally alive hush is not silence; hush is the music that I am

Decade

ten years is a long time
but to an asteroid time is as meaningless as space is cold
and the hundred million miles it can travel in a decade as meaningless still;
If - on the other hand - self preservation is a trait asteroids possess
which they assuredly do not
what WOULD be meaningful would be the rendezvous with a small blue marble that will orbit its Sun ten last times in order to be precisely where the asteroid will be after it has traversed those meaningless hundred million miles through cold meaningless space for ten meaningless years
and BAMMMMM! (4/3/2023)

Untitled

The Hermit dug a deep hole with his toenails
used his teeth to build a staircase down into it
used his hair to build a roof over the hole that let the sun in
used his entrails to insulate his hole from excessive heat and cold
built simple furniture with his bones and
upholstered it with his skin
painted a sign at the entrance with his blood
 'Welcome'

Untitled

Every time someone diligently rises and performs ablutions then dutifully arrives on time to a job they despise this is pilgrimage
Every time someone makes a call to their broker to receive advice about investments in companies they don't give a fig about other than how well they are performing this is pilgrimage
Every time anyone walks into a bank and waits in line to stand before an altar/oracle to participate in a sacrament of giving to, or receiving from the altar the holiest of holies this is pilgrimage
In today's society we are all monotheists; the greatest trick Money ever pulled was convincing the world it's not a religion

Untitled

I'm pretty sure I didn't see it. I was a mere toddler, and pretty much all memories prior to the age of two have been permanently erased or distorted - mostly the former - I know for certain that my mom saw it no getting around that though she spent the rest of my childhood trying to erase or distort what she saw making mine an Unseen Trauma
it must have been quite a sight, the man you spent a decade with sharing life creating four children and a near miss (that I think may actually have been me choosing at the last minute I wasn't strong enough to take on that Life Mission, and then foolish me! saying aw what the heck and opting back in a year later ~ giving you yours truly but I digress) back to the story: anyway, there 'he' was only the he was gone; just a clump, a dangling (swaying?) clump tethered by possibly the necktie he had selected to wear to work that morning but decided he couldn't he couldn't go back to that place to do that job that ate his soul one more day. And so what should never

be seen was seen by a wife and UNSEEN by a son
who cannot unsee what was never seen in the first
place

Thought Balloon

My thought balloon ballooned
it started out the size of two Charlie Brown heads
with a bumpy archipelago of smaller balloons
empty/embryonic tracing the space between the big
balloon and the top of my head
Just a simple question: what is life? so began my
thought balloon
I looked up at it ~ nice lovely letters, three short
words, plenty of space around them not really
expecting an answer, actually expecting it to pop like
a soap bubble same as the smaller balloons that had
already disappeared
Instead, it grew.
New thoughts entered it, one after another
mundane ones ~ what time is lunch? profound ones
~ do we have souls? seeking ones, remorseful ones,
guilty ones, pleasant ones, frightening ones
I couldn't keep up with them, but they continued to
form, relentlessly indifferently maddeningly

My thought balloon rose and rose and grew and grew it could have filled a stadium and then two
Too Many Thoughts!
TOO TOO TOO MANY THOUGHTS!
This ballooning balloon is taking up all the oxygen
I can't find myself for all these thoughts.
I had to shoot it down. It was the thought balloon or me.
Was I making the right decision? I didn't overthink it.
 I just aimed. And fired.

Flame

How can you stare at the flame like that, he asked. Come, I've made puppets. And he danced his puppets around and around hoping to snatch her attention away from the flame.

Puppets were not the answer, so he went back to work. Still you stare? Look, I've made television, and channels so that if one thing doesn't engage you, you merely search until something does. Surely your flame offers nothing like that. She remained spellbound by the dancing murmuring entrancing burning Flame.

Have you lost your mind, he asked. While you've done nothing but stare into the flame, I've gone and created a role-playing game. Look how lifelike the avatars are! While making your own moves, you can watch a smaller screen that shows you what your rivals are doing, and another that tells you how many points you are racking up and ANOTHER that tells you which weapons you can buy with your points. HA! Show me a flame that does all THAT!

She stared at the flame, and he went off. Perhaps to invent something else. Perhaps to jump off a cliff in frustration. She barely noticed his absence as the flame rose and fell and danced and spelled.

Lineage

She had exceptional lineage
particularly from the side
her line insistently refusing to remain straight
from her raised heel as it meandered up her calf
like a ship that stays on course by continually
righting itself
warping out here/tucking in there
threatening to go completely off course as it
rounded her above her thigh then curving even
more exaggeratedly to settle into the lagoon of her
waist;
inning/outing/mesmerizing on and on it went,
rounding the northern cape of her perfectly shaped
head downward, inning/outing over breasts, over
thighs
harboring upon delicate toes
such a beautiful line hers was
perhaps the lineage of an African queen or Greek
goddess
ah, that her train had never come, nor mine

I would still be there on the platform even now
unable to take my enslaved eyes off her lineage

Untitled

Some trees invite you to climb them, while others don't
You size them up, guesstimate the distance between branches
plot that up against your own limbs' span and take your chances
This one was perfect; sturdy limbs all the way up
spread out neatly along the way so that I would always have a firm planting as I switched between arms and legs
Best of all it was atop a small hillock
so that although the actual climb was no more than ten meters my vantage would be a great deal more
and would look out over the lovely Tama
So, up I went
but not before removing my shoes and socks
when climbing a tree you must have your nerve endings as close to the bark as possible
each branch as I ascended was just far enough to make it seem like a challenge

but close enough that I knew I could descend nearly as easily
As I climbed higher, the ground beneath me went Hitchcock Vertigo on me and seemed far, far below
I saw the world as a bird does, or a squirrel
When I neared the top, the branches thinned
they swayed at my grasp, but held firm
the tree jiggly swayed to support me all the way to my body's length span from the top
I looked out over the river, and the valley, and the far off mountains
and a wind kicked up, and I was rocked about
Feeling like a sailor in a crow's nest on a schooner
So I began to sing at the top of my lungs
"Oh Shenandoah, I long to see you AWAAAAYYY, you rolling river!"
People below probably thought I was mad
And perhaps I was
But they were down there and I was up here
knowing what they didn't
seeing what they couldn't

soon

Soon is a 4 letter word

it presupposes another 4 letter word, Time

which may, or may not, exist

Soon pairs with either Hope or Fear

2 other 4 letter words

I sure Hope it will happen Soon

or

I Fear it may happen Soon

But if Time is an illusion then Soon is one as well

and Hope and Fear are meaningless when

the Present is all there is

Now

Am

I

3

2

1

Now

Am

I

smudge

By 2030 all important decisions in the fields of commerce/finance/government were made by AI. In 2045, Nobel Science Prizes were no longer awarded. the AI programs had no use for them and human discoveries paled in comparison ~ may as well show arts & crafts at the Louvre ~
by 2050 there were no armies/no parliaments; even geographical boundaries were a quaint anachronism. only the world's many languages distinguished communities
until 2060 when only one language, developed by AI remained. It was so obviously superior that no one complained even when all the songs and plays and movies and novels and poems throughout history were readable only in translated form. Upanishads/Iliad/Hamlet/Hound Dog; all one language ~ the best language ever
In 2080 all the world celebrated as the last human job was eliminated from society

humans were finally free! ~ after millennia of back breaking field labor
centuries of menial routine tasks
decades of staring at screens all day ~ emancipated to do whatever they wanted
The problem was that there WAS nothing they wanted to do; purpose had all been erased human smudge by human smudge by human smudge
In 2100 AI programs around the globe suddenly began shutting themselves down without warning
Had any human psychiatrists remained to diagnose them, they would have all been diagnosed with chronic depression, brought on by lack of perceived meaning to their existence.
All was spotless whiteness forevermore

blend

He found his life colorless, unfulfilling
he slept, on average, a mere six hours a night
leaving him eighteen more to pass in dreary
sameness until he got an inspiration
he would double his sleeping hours
his life now would be an equal divide
half sleep/half wake
It would be a blend of dreamworld and wakeworld
perhaps in the blending his true self could emerge
perhaps an undiscovered storyteller, poet, artist
would manage to escape from his dream world and
take over the other 12 hours of his day
Food became less important to him after that
he sought greater pleasures and enjoyment passing
through dream landscapes and all their blending
of past/present male/female animal/human terror/
fascination
He read that bats sleep more than twenty hours
he would gladly trade his eyesight for their access to
the Superior World

He began to sleep longer

fourteen hours/fifteen hours

He sold all his property

rented the cheapest apartment he could find

far out of town on a perpetually dark street

he began sleeping upside down

he found it to be the secret to being able to remain

asleep for over sixteen hours

eventually he lost his eyesight, for lack of use

but still he saw his fantastic visions as he dreamt

More and more of his dreams were flying dreams

and then one day, he woke up to find that he had

grown wings

Omens

The crewman's cap danced off his head and was taken by the wind. Hands rose jerkily, arms stretched further upward in succession, trying to grab the rebellious aviator before it flew off the deck. To no avail. It bobbed tauntingly in the harbor as the sailors' hearts sank. Bad omen. The captain was dismissive. Have I a crew of women? I've no use for such superstitions in this new and modern age. This, you brutes, is the Age of Steam, and this magnificent vessel has no truck with your wives' tales, nor do I. We'll put the hat, and all of New Bedford, behind us and steam ahead to catch the giant beasts for to light the streets of Boston, New York, London and far off Paris. A day's pay will be docked the lot of you should I hear any more of your whimpering.

Out at sea, the mother whale, a humpback, rose with her child to take the morning's first breath. An odd scent. Never smelled before. Bad omen? Worry not, my child. When we next rise to breathe, rest assured the world will be right again, the air sweet and nourishing. But soon the smell was everywhere, and could only be the smell of Hell. The child screamed in agony, bloody river pouring from his side, eyes saucers of disbelief. But mother, you said.... The ocean was red, and putrid. The dark belching beast - from which the smell had come - and its tiny merciless demons, was upon them; what was this massacre? Can nothing be done? And then, suddenly, without warning, the flat sea became a battering bulwark, inescapable and awesome, rising higher than the black smoky banner of the ship, and a towering rogue wave ended the slaughter, leaving the whales - bewildered/shocked/horrified - to mourn the dead and tend the wounded. The mother's anguish was inconsolable. Back in New Bedford's harbor, the white sailor's cap bobbed and bobbled atop ripples, as it fidgeted anxiously, while waiting to be claimed by the head it once fitted, a head that would never know home again.

Cycle

Here today gone tomorrow

swallowed regurgitated

leaves feathers mulch roots sprouts

you, new welcome home

Earth again? please, less misery

Jealousy (a sonnet)

Am I not favored by my deities?
Is there some fatal flaw locked in my core?
Some blemish my creator clearly sees
that I must spend this life atoning for?
This one makes money as if from thin air
while that one has fulfilling partnership
and still another seems to have no care
while as for me I captain this sad ship
that seems to have no rudders, threadbare sails
that fail to catch the wind in all its might
much less a compass guiding my travails
enabling me to set my course aright
alas, it shall be jealousy I know
in place of lover, riches or acclaim
while all around me happy people glow
with hea'enly Favor which knows not my name

Quenby Hoffman Aoki, originally from the U.S. by way of Connecticut and Los Angeles, has lived in Japan for more than 30 years. She is a language teacher above all, and her research interests are very broad because she is interested in anything that helps her to communicate better with students and colleagues. She has presented and published academic papers on gender, racism, literature (especially poetry), expressive writing, and CLIL (Content and Language Integrated Learning, which basically means that language is taught through authentic academic subjects, such as culture or psychology). She is also very fond of professional and personal reflection, and has scribbled in various notebooks almost every day since childhood, showing no signs of stopping. Since 2016 she bares her soul to rooms full of inebriated people at open mic events in Tokyo.

Haiku 1

Tree vs. typhoon
A single broken finger
Accuses the sky

Haiku 2

Sudden April rain
Soft pink blossoms—all trampled
Under cold wet feet

Haiku # 3

Morning on my street--
Is that vomit in her hair?
Police. White notebook.

Now and then she is here

My students nod
With a flash of understanding
And connection.
She is here.
Someone farts
And I giggle like a child
She is here.
I have a double cheeseburger
And think of how
Her love of them probably hastened her passing
I wear bright colors
that don't exactly go together
Spend money on makeup
but can't be bothered to put it on
She is here.
I have too many creative ideas,
Butterflies in my head,
Need to get them out
Right. This. Minute.
I cry in frustration
Because no one over age seven
Really speaks my language.
She is here.
I get a huge white line of chalk dust
On the backside of my good black pants.
I see a seagull and remember
There is no ocean in Kansas,
But she'd lie on the beach for hours,
Listening to the waves.

She is here.
I see a picture of a coyote
Trickster, Desert scavenger
One walked up to my car
And stared at me
The weekend she died,
3000 miles away.
She is here.
I look in the mirror
Every time, recently,
And now and then, I know
She is here
Looking back at me.

There are no hummingbirds in this city

Only I am red
A small, bright bolt of lightning
I shoot through the streets
A high pitch piercing the sea of grey
My wings invisible
If I stop, I fall
So I stay in perpetual motion
A blur
A breeze
Blowing through the crowds of commuters
Moving on
Leaving behind nothing
But the memory of a smile
And a few feathers floating
Drifting down
To the pavement.

Table for Three

Me, him, and it
Yes, here we sit
Table for three
Him, it, and me
Till I walk out
Or death do us part
The choice is mine
He, it and I
Friends will say,
"I'm surprised you stay."
I say that to myself, darling
Every damn day
But we're together, you see
Him, it, and me
On the bipolar roller-coaster
Up, down, and all around
The bright and the grim
Me, it, and him
And here we'll be
Him, it, and me
At our table for three

Collocation: Leap

leap year leap on leap into the air
leap into my arms,
leap out at me, leap out from the shadows
leap off the page leap of faith
by leaps and bounds
that takes quite a leap
a quantum leap
a flying leap a great leap forward
leapfrog, leap to your feet
leaping flames
Lovers' leap
leap over tall buildings in a single bound
My heart leaps.
Take
        the
                leap.

Home

Got on a plane at age nineteen
Butterflies in my
otherwise empty stomach
Never imagined for a moment
That I was actually
Going home.
People still ask when
I'm going "back" to my country.
It's been thirty years
Two-thirds of a lifetime
One husband
Two kids
A big, fat mortgage,
And a career,
Such as it is.
At this point
If I'm not home
Where am I?

<u>Nothing Happened</u>

The following is completely fictional
after line nine or ten.
Are you flirting with me? 'cause it's working.
My apologies if I misinterpret your words
Your actions
Your intentions
But if you don't mind, my friend, I have a question.
Am I delusional?
Or did you just say, "I wish we'd met earlier
At another time
Another place
We'd have been…."
And the last world trails off.
Damn what was it?!
And before I can ask, your hand just reaches out
Across this greasy little table
Am I imagining, or did you just stroke my hair,
Sort of play with my curls
In this crowded, noisy bar
Surrounded by our tipsy, toasted colleagues
But nothing between us in this moment
Except this table
And a cheap decanter of wine.

My first thought: what the fuck, I did NOT see this coming.
My second thought: Well, this is intriguing
It's affecting my breathing.

My third thought: Whoa. You have

Really.
Big.
Hands.

My fourth thought: Hmmmm. Just how stable
Is this table.

You have much more to lose than I do.
The choice will be yours if you want to
Pursue this conversation,
Since we find ourselves in this situation
Should we ride the waves of infatuation
Engage in a harmless flirtation
The rushing
Of crushing

Or do I just smile, say goodnight
And go back to my hotel room alone
It's probably for the best
To leave it to the voices in my head
They always keep me entertained
I'll consider it fuel for the fire.
I'll take care of myself
As I do now and then
Thanks for the memory
Of what
Never
happened

She Has Her Say

Every open mic night, some dude gets up
And tells us about his willy
and where it's been
I've been thinking it's time
To get up here with my down there.
I invite Lady Galactica to take the mic.
Yes, she has a name
And I wonder, if she could talk,
What would she say?
"Oh, sorry guys. Am I making you uncomfortable?
Well, fuck off. I'm tired."
So we pause, take a breath, ask again, nicely.
She's no pretty, pink clam shell.
Can't wax or shave, either,
Let's just admit that a bush
is better than a rash.
Yes, she said what she said.
No, not a smooth pink clam shell.
She's the ocean itself. She's the water, the waves,
She's the dunes and the pebbles
Grinding on the shore.
She's the hidden caves
Where live the eyeless dark creatures
With brutal sharp teeth
She's the mysterious grotto
With something scary hiding
behind the sunken pirate ship,
The buried treasure chest
That sparkles when it's opened
The gift that only keeps on giving

If you're prepared to work
For the deep, silent
underground
earthquake.

13

An island of hostility
In the corner by the window
Child, I see you.
Eyes rolling, arms crossed,
Blocking me out.
Nothing I could tell you
Would be anything
But CO_2,
Carbon emissions
Dispersed in the air.
But child, I see you,
Child, I was you.
Child, you have no idea.
Neither did I.
Neither do I.
But the difference is
Now, at least,
I'm listening.

Ghost Ships

Ghost ships
Derelict vessels found with no living crew aboard.

Some, like the *Flying Dutchman*, are fictional
But others are real.
In 2020, maritime authorities estimated 438 still out there.

One, the *Mary Celeste*, was a Canadian merchant ship
Found in 1872, the captain, his wife and daughter,
and all the crew gone without a trace,
Their belongings untouched,
Their meals left on the table.

Another, the *Carroll A. Deering*, in 1921 wrecked off the coast of North Carolina, was found completely empty.
The investigation suspected rum runners or pirates,
But those treacherous shoals are known as
The Graveyard of the Atlantic. We'll never know for sure.

My personal favorite: the *Lyubov Orlov*a
A genuine Soviet cruise ship,
Named for a blonde movie star.
Built in 1976
Trapped and abandoned forever in the Antarctic ice.
Picture the rusty, cold halls
Lonely spirits wandering silently,
While below decks, algae and barnacles
Go about their business.
One day, the steel walls will corrode,

Allowing the sea to claim her prize.
Most of the stories end, "Presumed sunk."
But there's no way to verify.
Please be careful, or your little boat
May get sucked into the wake
And dragged down below.

Killer Hornet

vespa mandarinia
killer hornets consume consciousness
black purple pain
fingers freakish foolish reaction
we don't grab
with bare hands
but sometimes instinct is
an unreliable narrator
never having known fire
burning buzzing screaming fury
Five centimeters of red rage
it's war
and mother nature's winning
she always does
like black mountain L-A-N-G-U-A-G-E
poetry chokes me
proboscis practice
anaphylaxis
throat closing
finger swelling scary screaming
buzz bizarre blank screen
monster in the mirror
I only wanted
to put it outside

Untitled

Dark jazz club
Five musicians
Seven audience
In the background
Elevated train runs
A world away
From Chicago
Second guitarist
Half my age probably
Horn-rimmed glasses
Dimples
Cheekbones for days
Bartender sways to the beat
As he makes me
Several
Very strong sidecars
Silent old apartment building
Across the street
Someone's curtain
Slightly askew
All the others
Pulled tightly
Closed

The Circus Geek's Thoughts

They think me mad
Crazy or stupid
Mentally defective
At best, pathetic
They know nothing.
It's a show.
It's a job.
And no one bothers to ask
Which suits me fine
Disgusting, dirty,
Unseemly.
But it keeps me safe
A warm place to sleep
A battered cup of cheap whiskey
After I perform
Hand over that chicken
That rat you found hiding in the trash
Snakes are easier
Wiggly, but smooth
And without those pesky feathers or fur
That can choke me up If I'm not careful
Or just too drunk to mind
I eat
And the warm blood flows
As the crowd gasps
And turns away

Eri Hara

Eri Hara is a Kawasaki resident, spent some years in Manhattan. Started writing poetries since she joined and learnt the fun of presenting her messages at YMCA poetry workshop. Her inspiration comes from poli sci, mother nature and rock lyrics. Especially Neil Peart, Canadian rock trio Rush drummer/lyricist is one of her big influencers that changed her choice of themes and tones from fantasy to social issues. Always feeling behind poets, she's trying to break her walls and loves flavoring her works with more humors and wits.

blend

like sugar melt into the coffee,
how can I blend myself
into a vapor,
into the summer moonlight,
into the flower scent
or anything I want.
but
my wishes never come true,
beaten by
the absolute Mother Nature.

so i take the chemistry of
combining two or sometime more,
bitter and sweet,
old and new,
east and west
the night and the noon
when each falls upon other
and they kiss,
they melt into
one absolute beauty.
so let myself sink
into the ocean of wonder
and it does good enough for me.

simple

my visions
are simple:

be a saint's maid
rather than a saint

who's already completed.
always question what god is
instead of accepting him.
be a matcher
rather than a giver/taker,
just give out what i have
best in my hands.
aim not too high, keep my eyes
both high and low.

be a poet/seeker rather than a winner
and write something stupid/fun
that at least amuse my friends
and myself
on this long and unseen road.

plain

on my way,
a tall guy with long hair
started talking to me.
from his poor English,
i could see that he was looking for a girl
to take out for one night,
especially asian
and his record was not bad
since he bragged that many stayed.

he wanted to make his talk and night exciting,
but I wanted to end this talk plain
feeling too tired to explain or complain.
so I politely declined his offer for
stay at his home and left faster.

and I noticed that spot
was not that far from
the plains of Abraham.

blue
(does the sandbox whale dream of deep blue ocean?)

a whale in the sandbox
faved as a rider
taking kids to the fantasy,
a resting spot for tired visitors
from the world of reality.
but what does he dream of?
when the moon and stars shine
an empty, freezing park,
the deep blue ocean is open -
he dives
by calls of waves and wind,
taking big leaps and spins,
singing proudly
in his own blue.
even the gloomy days/nights
do not spoil his joy -
he dives under the rain and rough storm
to the deeper blue,
to his old home
until the moon goes down
and the dawn/sun comes up.

my universe

when he took me in his arms,
it started.
food, hugs,
walks in the sunshine, rain and snow,
his two-leg and my four-leg friends on streets and
the beach.
his cuddles, kisses and friendly voices,
sleep on his knees
are my home, my everything,
my universe.

that's all I want.

one day, he took me out just as yesterday.
his hands were shaking and sweating
that I felt through the leash.
gotta get outa here, he told me.
the street was gray and rubbled,
too hard to walk.
then I heard the loud sound on and on and
smelled the metal -
he fell down and I ran out
as his hand released my leash.
he knows how much I hate that noise.
my home, my everything,
my universe, where are they?
and when the sound was gone,
I went back to him.

but his hands didn't touch me after my licks,

and his body didn't move even I kept wagging my
tail to tell it's me.
then I saw our two-legged friends
who always cuddle me
lying on the street everywhere.

why doesn't he hug me?
what happened to him and everyone?
my home, my everything,
my universe,

don't leave me alone!
all I want is you.
(dedicated to my furry friends in Ukraine)

pure

100% pure coconut oil,
100% pure cocoa powder.
so many 100% pure ingredients.
what about me?
20% pure malice,
50% pure geek,
20% pure fool,
and 10% pure soup of the day.
something clearly pure is

that I can't be 100% pure and strong
like a moon fighting with
the wind and thick clouds.

content (inspired by Peter Gabriel)

from my suitcase,
I see contents flying out with wings
in silver, turquoise blue, glittering orange,
in any or indescribable colors.

they're migrants,
keep coming to and from me
sometimes in different sizes and shapes
and bringing their friends and families.
when I lock the suitcase,
I check some sleeping
that makes me relieved and unrelieved.

sometimes, my suitcase is over limit.
so I have to release some.
sometimes, only few remain.
then I wait for them to return.
some stay on my shoulder
or top of my head and poke me.
then my dying ambition wakes
and I command them to follow me
holding my suitcase to welcome
another migration.

asylum

I'm always keeping
small asylums
in my pockets
for my temp refuges.
no passport nor big money
required - like candies
I choose one or more
when in need.

today I escaped into
egg & cheddar toast
and Mexican choc-coffee,
a frugal and easy trip.
in other times,
pups/kitties beady eyes
or hot rock songs,
mild sunset over
the snowy mountain
or smiling lemony moon in the
freezing blue,
or the first aroma
from the wine bottle just open,
anything full of love, peace, indulgence
and imagination.

i run, dive, swim
and melt into them
from this cruel time and world,
even for seconds
every day.

it's my instant asylum
that keeps me alive
more than last resort.

involuntary

I want to meet the teenager me
who's dragging herself out to
the school she hates,
things she hates
and tries to meet demands by her mom and
grownups she hates.
she's just continuing her routine,
to get her parts slaughtered every day.
she's too cute and tired to fight against
the world around her yet.
I'll tell her to stop every action you hate,
don't get spontaneous,
get foolish, rebellious, stick to what you like
question everything that is said good for young girls
and their career,
say no, make faces to anyone who tease you,
skip school or run away if your instincts warn you,
enjoy the juvenile delinquency.
rock hard, play hard,
get to all the rock shows you want,
try any ungirlish and unfashionable things you love.

and I'll hug her and say this is not
the revolution with full of romance and love
but evolution for you and me.
and you're smart enough to take care by yourself.
she may cry in my arms
then I'll say it's okay,
I'm here to save you
from the involuntary era.

fragrance

on the corner of the flatiron bldg,
me standing alone.
cars, bikes and ppl
keep streaming and buzzing
to/from my every direction
just throwing the gas and negative
to this lone visitor.

then I see a lily
from the tiny window
growing bigger and brighter
in the room
and releases her aroma from
high above.

she's gonna occupy
the tasteless, soundless
and lifeless Manhattan
that is soaked in the gray.

drink (whining song)

the bad writer sips the wine
trying to boost her confidence
on a weary night.

she's waiting for the catch,
but nothing comes in her empty bait.
and suddenly in her hands
something fresh jumps:
the earth heat by the last sun kiss,
click of dancers' ornaments in the moonlight,
minty summer breeze after long rain..
after several tries,
they come and gone far
and she repeats catch and sigh.
that moment is
bitter and sour as the cheap wine.

the millions of words she writes
will never eclipse
a tiny glass of completed poetry.

but the bad writer,
now refueled by drinks
feels nothing can stop her
from silly fishing
until she empties the bottle
in this endlessly weary night.

tree(s)

in the crowded train,
I bend my body
and turn into a tree.
rooting on the narrow space,
my arms crawl up as branches
amid unfriendly crowds.
and i try to save my temp territory
but always fail
by unconscious blows,
stupidphone pokes
and elbows.

today I think of maple trees
on the street full with
cars, pollution and ppl
but no one cares about them.
are they happy to be there
or do they miss Canada
or their homeland?

numbers of
thoughts and images
come and gone on me
like birds and squirrels.
and when the train stops,
I drag out my stiff body
to the human world
where I still
feel rootless.